Leading for Success

**Unleash your leadership potential to achieve
extraordinary results**

Soft Skills for
IT Professionals

Leading for Success

Unleash your leadership potential to achieve extraordinary results

SARAH COOK

Soft Skills for
IT Professionals

IT Governance Publishing

IT Governance Publishing
IT Governance Limited
Unit 3, Clive Court
Bartholomew's Walk
Cambridgeshire Business Park
Ely
Cambridgeshire
CB7 4EH
United Kingdom

www.itgovernance.co.uk

First published in the United Kingdom in 2009
by IT Governance Publishing.

ISBN 978-1-905356-92-8

FOREWORD

IT is often seen as a 'hard-skill' profession where there is no place for soft skills. Yet the importance of soft skills for the IT professional should not be underrated; they underlie all behaviours and interactions. Both IT and non-IT professionals need to work together and learn from each other for effective business performance. All professionals, be they in IT or elsewhere, need to understand how their actions and reactions impact on their behaviour and working relationships.

This series of books aims to provide practical guidance on a range of soft-skills areas for those in IT and also for others, including those who deal with IT professionals, in order to facilitate more effective and co-operative working practices.

Each book is written by an experienced consultant and trainer. Their approach throughout is essentially practical and direct, offering a wealth of tried and tested professional guidance. Each chapter contains a diagnostic and focused questions to help the manager plan and steer their course. The language used is jargon-free, and a bibliography and a helpful glossary of terms are included at the end of the book.

Angela Wilde, February 2009

PREFACE

This book is intended to provide IT managers with practical advice and tips on how to become an effective leader. Whatever the environment in which you work, providing effective leadership leads to a climate where team members want to give of their best and where organisational goals are more likely to be reached. Furthermore, there is a strong link between leadership and the creation of the stakeholder value of an organisation.

Gone are the days when leadership was merely a quality that people at the top of the organisation needed to demonstrate. In order to succeed today organisations need distributed leadership. This is leadership that is demonstrated at every level throughout the business.

Whether you are new to leadership, or have been a leader for some time, this book will help you to develop your leadership skills. It is designed to assist you in understanding what the characteristics are of an effective leader, to help you assess where your strengths and development areas are and to aid you in creating a plan of action for realising your leadership potential.

I hope that you will find this book informative and practical and that it provides you with details on how you can become an even more effective leader.

Sarah Cook

The Stairway Consultancy Ltd

www.thestairway.co.uk

ABOUT THE AUTHOR

Sarah Cook is the Managing Director of the Stairway Consultancy Ltd. She has 15 years' consulting experience specialising in leadership and management development, team building and change. Prior to this, Sarah worked for Unilever and as Head of Customer Care for a retail marketing consultancy.

As well as having practical experience of helping individuals to improve their leadership skills, Sarah is a business author and has written widely on leadership and management development, team development and coaching. She also speaks regularly at conferences and seminars on these topics.

Sarah is a Fellow of the Chartered Institute of Personnel and Development and a Chartered Marketeer. She has an MA from Cambridge University and an MBA. Sarah is an accredited user of a wide range of psychometric and team diagnostic tools. She may be contacted via *sarah@ thestairway.co.uk*.

ACKNOWLEDGEMENTS

I wish to acknowledge:

R. R. Blake and J. S. Mouton, *The Managerial Grid*, Gulf Publishing, 1964.

R. R. Blake and J. S. Mouton, *The New Managerial Grid*, Gulf Publishing, 1978.

S. Cook, S. Macaulay and H. Coldicott, *Change Management Excellence*, Kogan Page, 2004.

J. Gardner, *On Leadership*, Free Press, 1993.

P. Hersey, *The Situational Leader*, Pfeiffer and Co, 1984.

P. Hersey and K. H. Blanchard, *The Management of Organizational Behaviour*, 8th edition, Prentice Hall, 2000.

CONTENTS

INTRODUCTION

This book is dedicated to IT professionals who want to improve their leadership skills.

No matter what environment people work in, team members look to a leader to motivate and inspire them to give of their best. Whether your business is in a phase of growth, facing a harsh economic climate or experiencing change, an effective leader rallies others to achieve organisational goals.

I particularly like a quote from Rosalynn Carter which I believe sums up effective leadership: 'A leader takes people where they want to go. A great leader takes people where they don't necessarily want to go, but ought to be'.

This book provides practical advice and proven techniques to help you enhance your leadership skills. It will help you better understand yourself and your business as well as other people. In doing so you can become a better leader.

You will find exercises and assessment tools, as well as theory on how to manage others effectively. Each chapter provides examples and ideas that you can readily put into practice.

CHAPTER 1: WHAT IS LEADERSHIP?

In this chapter I provide:

- A description of what makes a great leader.
- An outline of the difference between leading and managing.
- A self-assessment tool for finding whether you spend most of your time managing or leading, and the implications of that for you, your colleagues and your customers.

What makes a great leader?

I was working in a business recently that had undergone a lot of change. Morale in the organisation was poor and there was uncertainty about the future. There was generally a stale air about the place and productivity was low.

There were several departments, however, including IT, where the atmosphere was entirely different. People in these departments had a buzz about them, they talked positively about the future and appeared energised and enthused. I left the IT department wondering what was so different about the people there. They were working in the same conditions and had undergone the same changes.

The key difference for each of these departments was that they had strong leaders in place. They had created an environment for their people where they wanted to give of their best, to go above and beyond the call of duty, in spite of the difficult circumstances.

1: What Is Leadership?

You will have your own experiences of great leaders – either those you've seen from afar or those you've worked closely with. If you take a few minutes to think about those people, to identify exactly what it is that makes them great leaders, you'll probably pick certain characteristics, such as that a great leader:

- is an effective communicator,
- is passionate,
- demonstrates integrity,
- challenges the status quo,
- is visionary,
- is motivational and
- is charismatic.

One management psychologist, John Gardner, studied a large number of leaders. He came to the conclusion that there were some qualities or attributes of leaders that suggested that a leader in one situation could lead in another. These included:

- energy and stamina,
- courage and resolution,
- trustworthiness,
- decisiveness,
- self-confidence,
- assertiveness,
- intelligence and an orientation towards action,
- eagerness to accept responsibility,
- ability to undertake a task,
- drive for achievement,

- awareness of the needs of followers,
- skill in dealing with people,
- capacity to motivate people and
- adaptability and flexibility.

However, researchers who followed Gardner challenged this list and it is certainly not exhaustive. One thing that is agreed is that in order to be an effective leader you need to have followers. Followers are inspired by what leaders know (about themselves, other people, the business, the competitive environment, and so on) and what they do, but above all by how they *are*, by their very being, modelling the role of a leader with total integrity and intuitively behaving like one.

The following triangle depicts this dynamic: being, knowing, doing.

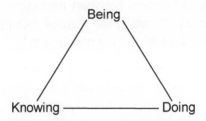

Figure 1: Being, knowing, doing

One definition of leadership is that leadership is about influencing others to achieve organisational goals. The effective leader takes people to places that they did not know they wanted to go themselves.

In order to do this, they need to have a strong sense of who they are, as well as a clear vision for the future. Business author Warren Bennis says, 'Leadership is a function of knowing yourself, having a vision that is well communicated, building trust among colleagues, and taking effective action to realise your own leadership potential.'

So shouldn't it just be senior managers at the top of the organisation that need leadership skills, rather than departmental managers?

Leading versus managing

Elisabeth Moss Kanter is a Professor at Harvard Business School who specialises in change. Her view is that change is now a fact of life for all businesses. She says that in changing times, not only is stronger leadership required, but also more leaders.

This means that managers at all levels of the organisation need to demonstrate leadership qualities. So let's start by looking at the difference between managing and leading – what it is that we do when we manage as opposed to what we do when we lead in an IT environment.

This is not a question of your title – for example you may be called a 'manager' or a 'team leader' – it's a question about what a manager or a leader does, about what behaviours they display.

So where do managers tend to focus their attention? This tends to be around setting objectives, monitoring, setting procedures, getting things done, ensuring that effective processes and procedures are in place.

And what about leaders? Leaders focus more on inspiring, setting strategies for the future, role modelling, coaching others to reach their potential, empowering others.

One of the key differences is the focus of manager behaviour on the here and now, on getting things done. The focus for the leader is on the future, on looking for different ways of doing things. This is a proactive approach as opposed to a reactive one.

Leader	**Manager**
Inspires Produces change Is boundless	Controls Produces predictability Is bounded
↓ **Change**	↓ **Maintenance**

Figure 2: Leading versus managing

Self-assessment – where do you spend your time?

Imagine there is a continuum, with managing on one end and leading on the other – where would you plot yourself, bearing in mind the activities you do and get involved in on a daily basis?

Considerable leadership

Considerable management

Figure 3: Where do you focus your efforts?

What are the consequences of where we focus our attention?

Let's look first at what happens if the amount of time we spend on leadership and the amount of time we spend on management are out of balance. In other words, a team has strong management and weak leadership. This is what we are likely to see:

Short term	→	Predictable performance
Low risk	→	Lack of innovation
Compliance	→	Low adaptability
Predictability	→	Slow to change
Bureaucratic	→	Lack of empowerment

Figure 4: Strong management and weak leadership

Conversely, if a team has strong leadership and weak management, these are the potential consequences:

Long term	→	Adaptable to market
Energetic	→	Lack of consistency
Just do it	→	Poor planning
Empowered	→	Minimal control
Individualistic	→	Lack of collaboration

Figure 5: Strong leadership and weak management

So when should we lead and when should we manage?

Let's look at the dynamics that tell us whether we should be managing or leading in our business environment. The following diagram shows two axes: the x-axis represents the complexity of your operation. In other words, the range of products and services that you offer and the number of different places where your organisation interfaces with the customer. The y-axis represents the degree of change that a market sector is experiencing.

Amount of change	High	Considerable leadership and little management	Considerable leadership and management
	Low	Little leadership or management	Considerable management and little leadership
		Low High	
		Complexity of operation	

Figure 6: Leadership versus management matrix

You will see from the matrix that considerable leadership and little management would work for a small, highly motivated group of people – perhaps a company that does a lot of research and development or innovation.

Little leadership and little management would work for a small-business owner offering one product or service in a market place where there is little change, such as window cleaning or car valeting.

Considerable management and little leadership would work in a production or manufacturing environment where there is a lot of emphasis on managing processes or production and where there is little change, such as a stationary company, getting the same sort of supplies from A to B.

Considerable leadership and considerable management would work well in any organisation where there is a large amount of change and the complexity of the operation is high, such as air travel, insurance, banking, the car industry, the leisure industry, the IT industry, and so on.

I am not saying here that managing is bad and leading is good. What I am trying to emphasise is that in the IT environment, you will need to be both an effective manager and an effective leader. The problem for most individuals is ensuring the balance and being clear when to manage and when to lead. As the business writer Steven Covey so aptly puts it, 'Management is efficiency in climbing the ladder of success; leadership determines whether the ladder is leaning against the right wall.' The following chapters provide you with practical advice on how to be a better leader in order to influence positively your team in order to achieve organisational goals.

Activities to undertake with your team

In order to increase your understanding of what others see as effective leadership, I suggest that you ask your team members what they see as the characteristics of great leaders. Discuss with them and your colleagues the differences they see between leading and managing and how this applies in your organisational context.

Summary

This chapter has provided you with a description of what makes a great leader and an outline of the difference between leading and managing. I have also encouraged you to assess whether you spend most of your time managing or leading or both, and the implications of that on you, your colleagues and your customers.

1: What Is Leadership?

Here are some questions to ask yourself after reading this chapter:

- Given your organisational and market environment, where should be the emphasis on leadership and management be for you?
- What can you do to redress the balance, if required?
- What do you need to do more of or do differently?
- How do you currently rate yourself against the characteristics of a good leader?
- What is a key area of strength for you in terms of leadership? What is an area that you need to develop further?

CHAPTER 2: LEADERSHIP STYLES

In this chapter I provide:

- A description of what leadership means in practice, using two contrasting models of leadership.
- A self-assessment questionnaire that will show you your leadership style preferences and their consequences.

Leadership in practice

We looked in the last chapter at what leadership is and when it is appropriate to use it. We also began by looking at the traits that great leaders demonstrate. This is follows one of the various theories of leadership that attempt to identify the common traits possessed by successful leaders. However, the list is ever-growing and no definitive list is possible.

Below I discuss two models – the support and challenge model and the leadership adaptability model – that shed light on which styles of leadership are best to use, and how and when to use them. I am not suggesting that either model is better than the other. The purpose of outlining both is for you to reflect on your own style of leadership.

The support and challenge leadership model

Robert Blake and Jane Mouton from Ohio State University and Michigan University developed an analysis of leadership called the leadership grid, outlining whether the leader is focused more on production and tasks or on relationships and people. The support and challenge model that we will now investigate builds on this. It suggests that an effective leader needs to provide support to their team, and also to challenge them.

When a leader provides support to their team, this involves:

- offering motivational feedback,
- listening,
- empathising,
- assisting,
- showing understanding,
- providing advice, guidance and back-up,
- giving permission to act,
- actively helping with resources and
- providing their own time and effort.

When a leader provides challenge, this can mean:

- offering developmental feedback,
- asking others to do better, through both the requests you make of them and the challenges you set them,
- questioning them, getting them to rethink their actions and decisions,
- offering alternatives,
- setting stretching targets,
- stating positive and negative consequences of actions and
- confronting underperformance assertively.

		High support	High support
Support	High	Low challenge **Counsellor**	High challenge **Coach**
	Low	Low support Low challenge **Abdicator**	Low support High challenge **Task Master**
		Low High	
		Challenge	

Figure 7: The support and challenge model

As you will see from this model, different mixes of support and challenge can lead to very different styles of leadership:

- High challenge and low support – Task Master.
- High support and low challenge – Counsellor.
- Low challenge and low support – Abdicator.
- High challenge and high support – Coach.

The leader's style will potentially create the following environments:

- High challenge and low support – stress.
- High support and low challenge – comfort-zone.
- Low challenge and low support – apathy.
- High challenge and high support – high-performance.

This model implies that high support and high challenge will therefore generally lead to high performance. However, this will vary in different situations and with different individuals, as we will see later in this chapter.

If the level of challenge is too low, we need additional challenge to stimulate higher performance. If the level of challenge is too high, we need support to reduce it to a manageable level.

Check your understanding of the support and challenge model

To bring this model to life, here is a quiz for you to complete. It is based on what four different leaders say they do when leading their team. Look at the four different situations identified in each scenario, and identify which scenario relates to which leadership style. Check your own answers with the suggested answers at the end of this chapter.

- Scenario 1
  - I tend to leave my team to their own devices.
  - I seek to maintain a steady pace of work with my team.
  - I drive my team hard to achieve their goals.
  - I am supportive of my team.
- Scenario 2
  - I avoid conflict at all cost.
  - I try to avoid conflict, but if it occurs I try to smooth things over in a friendly way.
  - When there is conflict I defend my position with counter-arguments.

- When there is conflict I keep calm and try to develop a joint solution.
- Scenario 3
  - My style could be described as counselling.
  - My style could be described as defensive.
  - My style could be described as *laissez-faire*.
  - My style could be described as consultative.
- Scenario 4
  - I rarely give feedback on others' performance.
  - I find it easy to give motivational feedback.
  - I tell people how they can improve.
  - My feedback is a balance of motivational and developmental advice.
- Scenario 5
  - I place high value on maintaining good relations.
  - I tend to do my own thing.
  - I search for workable solutions.
  - I tend to impose my decisions.
- Scenario 6
  - I use humour to maintain friendly situations or when there is disagreement, to shift things away from serious discussion.
  - My humour can be seen by others as rather pointless.
  - My humour is hard-hitting.
  - My humour fits the situation and I retain a sense of humour even under pressure.

Rate your own leadership style

I have designed this questionnaire so that you can rate your own leadership style. You can also ask your team members to provide feedback on your leadership style by asking them the same questions. You can then compare and contrast the scores.

When you complete this questionnaire about yourself, be honest.

If you do not have team members, answer the questions in relation to how you deal with your colleagues.

Thinking about yourself as a leader, rate how characteristic the following behaviours are of you. Give each statement a score on a scale of:

1 = Totally uncharacteristic; you do this less than 10% of the time.

2 = Not characteristic; you do this up to 30% of the time.

3 = Not very characteristic; you do this up to 50% of the time.

4 = Somewhat characteristic; you do this up to 70% of the time.

5 = Characteristic; you do this up to 90% of the time.

6 = Totally characteristic; you do this up to 100% of the time.

Use the score sheet following the questionnaire to record your answers.

1   I praise others for a job well done.

2   I set others stretching goals.

3 I provide support for my team members when they need it.

4 I question others' approach to tasks and the impact of their actions.

5 I involve my team in decision making.

6 I tell my team members which areas they need to improve in.

7 I listen to others' points of view.

8 I set targets for individuals' development.

9 I encourage my team to do a good job.

10 I suggest alternative ways of doing things.

11 I ask my team members for their ideas.

12 I drive my team to constantly seek improvement.

13 I encourage others to work as a team.

14 My priority is for my team members to achieve targets.

15 I am approachable.

16 I expect high standards in others.

17 I provide team members with guidance and advice.

18 I tackle poor performance appropriately.

19 I am interested in my team members as individuals.

20 I state my expectations of my team members.

21 I build the confidence of others through praise.

22 I build team members' competence through pointing out gaps in their skills.

23 I value others' input.

24 I tell my team members if they are going off track.

25 I am considerate.

26 I like to raise the bar.

27 I make use of the strengths of my team members.

28 I am up front about my team members' weaknesses.

29 I ask others how things should be done.

30 I tell others how things should be done.

Scoring

Transfer your scores to the grid below.

Question	Score	Question	Score
1		2	
3		4	
5		6	
7		8	
9		10	
11		12	
13		14	
15		16	
17		18	
19		20	
21		22	
23		24	

25		26	
27		28	
29		30	
Total this column for support		**Total this column for challenge**	

Table 1: Score grid

Now place your total scores for support and the total scores for challenge in the appropriate boxes on the grid below. Mark where the two scores meet.

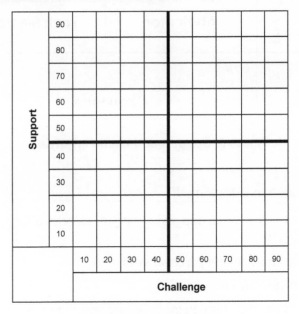

Figure 8: Score matrix

Next, look at which of the four boxes the scores lie in. Refer to the diagram below to find which leadership style you adopt. So, for example, if your two scores meet in the top left quadrant of the score matrix, your style is Counsellor; the top right quadrant, Coach; the bottom left quadrant, Abdicator; and the bottom right quadrant, Task Master.

Support	High	High support Low challenge **Counsellor**	High support High challenge **Coach**
	Low	Low support Low challenge **Abdicator**	Low support High challenge **Task Master**
		Low High	
		Challenge	

Figure 9: Support and challenge styles

Questions to ask yourself

- What is the leadership style that you identified for yourself?
- Is this how others perceive your style?
- How do you know this?
- What are the consequences of you adopting this style?

The consequences of support and challenge leadership styles

Let's look at the consequence of the leadership style that you adopt. Have you ever wondered why people are sometimes not performing to their full potential – even when you've tried to understand where they are coming from and what the issues are? Our normal reaction is to look at their skills and knowledge.

However, just as important are the attitude and energy that they demonstrate towards their work. High-performing individuals have a positive attitude combined with high energy, which results in them taking action and having a positive impact on their colleagues and customers and on the business.

Figure 10 is a behaviour model that will help you to think about where your team are and how they are performing. The model illustrates simple behavioural patterns that can be seen in people at work. These behaviours depend on the degrees to which individuals have a positive attitude and invest energy into their everyday activities.

Here is a brief description of the behaviours you may see in people in your team in the following areas:

- The Audience
  - o display positive attitudes and low energy;
  - o acknowledge good ideas but are themselves reluctant to change;
  - o avoid taking risks and keep a low profile; and
  - o try to ride things out until things return to normal.

		The Audience	High Performers
Attitude	Positive	Positive about what is happening Reluctant to get involved Threatened when too exposed Comfortable to watch from sidelines Reluctant to take risks	Feel challenged and stretched Comfortable with the need for change Open to possibilities and ideas In control of their own destiny Optimistic about the long-term future
		The Disengaged	**Sceptics**
	Negative	Unhappy and/or depressed Bruised self-esteem Overwhelmed by work Feeling powerless Fearing mistakes	Not listened to; excluded, constrained Rebellious, determined to block change they do not own Angry at the world for ignoring them Frustrated Overtly confident in their own ability
		Low High	
		Energy	

Figure 10: Followers' behaviour

- Sceptics
  - display negative attitudes and high energy;
  - express frustration over pain and the hesitancy of others;
  - argue against changes and always see the negatives;
  - press for quick solutions and decisive actions, and then criticise them; and
  - are oblivious to the consequences of their negativity.
- The Disengaged
  - display negative attitudes and low energy;
  - block out challenges;
  - avoid confronting issues;
  - retreat into 'safety', burying their heads in the sand;
  - avoid risk, doing the minimum; and
  - avoid thinking about what might happen.
- High Performers
  - display positive attitude and high energy;
  - see the silver lining hidden within the dark clouds;
  - view ambiguity and change as a challenge and an opportunity;
  - perform well, no matter what the circumstances;
  - treat life as a continuous learning experience; and
  - expand their personal comfort zone.

How do the behaviours of followers relate to your leadership style? If you look back at the four leadership styles of the support and challenge model, you will find that the way you behave has direct consequences in how your followers behave. So, for example,

- If you are a Coach, you are likely to encourage high performance.

- If you are a Counsellor, you are likely to encourage audience-type behaviour.

- If you are an Abdicator, you encourage people to become disengaged.

- If you are a Task Master, you potentially encourage sceptics.

We have a responsibility as leaders to challenge our own behaviour. The ideal way to create a climate where people give of their best is to demonstrate behaviours associated with the Coach, thereby acting as a role model of the behaviours we expect of others.

As leaders it is our role is to continue to challenge these behaviours every day, as positive attitudes and high energy will lead to high performance in most circumstances.

The leadership adaptability model

We've all been in situations where things have gone differently to the way we expected them to go. Perhaps you've given an individual plenty of freedom and delegated responsibility, but the outcome is not what you wanted – they've gone off in the wrong direction. The leadership adaptability model implies that one style doesn't always suit all people and situations.

Hersey and Blanchard identified four different leadership styles that can be drawn upon to deal with contrasting situations. Their theory is useful in increasing your awareness of the need to adapt your leadership style according to the willingness and ability of the team member in question.

The four leadership styles that they identified can be described as:

- Directing: this style or approach is characterised by giving a great deal of direction to subordinates and by devoting considerable attention to defining roles and goals.
- Guiding: while most of the direction is given by the leader, there is an attempt at encouraging people to 'buy into' the task.
- Supporting: decision making is shared between leaders and followers – the main role of the leader being to facilitate and communicate.
- Delegating: the leader still identifies the problem or issue, but the responsibility for carrying out the response is given to followers.

So when is it appropriate to use which style?

Assuming that you have passed your driving test, can you remember what it was first like to learn to drive a car? What happened to your confidence (willingness) and competence (ability) as you were learning?

You could say that before getting into the car you were willing to have a go – let's face it, you wouldn't have got in otherwise. But at the same time you are clearly not able to drive a car. At this stage, therefore, you are willing and not able. You are keen and eager but just a beginner.

You then get into the car and your instructor begins to explain all the things you need to do. Check your mirrors, check you are in neutral, and so on. All of a sudden you are aware of everything you need to learn and may be scared of failure, or worried about looking stupid if you do things wrong. At this stage, you may well find that you have become not so willing – and certainly not able. You become cautious and you are aware of what you can't do or don't know.

You overcome this – for some that happens more quickly than for others – and continue with your lessons until you get to the stage where you pass your test! You are now able to drive, but when it comes to going out for the first time – or getting onto the motorway – you may not be so keen to go out on your own. At this stage, you are not so willing, but hey, you've passed your test and you're able! Yet you still have trepidations; you're careful and reluctant.

Finally, you reach the stage where you're completely willing and very able to drive around safely. You're a high performer. Yet when you do something frequently, you often find that old habits creep in; this is where you may still need someone to help point these out and coach you to improve your performance continually.

How would you treat someone who is completely new to a job, as opposed to someone who has been doing the job for some time and is performing well?

Thinking about this scenario, you can see that people need different levels of direction and support at different stages. Clearly, when you start to learn something, you need a great deal of direction. However, once you are willing and able, you can go ahead on your own, supported by focused coaching to keep you on track and improve your performance.

The key to all this is identifying where an individual is in their development and adapting your leadership style, based on them and their situation. Everyone is different and we all go at different paces; some people may stay at one stage longer than others, so treat each task or situation differently.

The following model summarises the four stages and appropriate leadership styles to use.

Willingness		Low Ability	High Ability
High		How do you feel? Keen to have a go, unaware of the 'unknown' **Appropriate leadership style – Directive**	How do you feel? Keen and competent **Appropriate leadership style – Delegating and Coaching**
Low		How do you feel? Out of comfort zone **Appropriate leadership style – Guiding**	How do you feel? Apprehensive and cautious **Appropriate leadership style – Supportive**
		Low	High
		Ability	

Figure 11: Levels of willingness and ability

1 Willing but not able – Directive style.

- Do:
  - o Provide clear direction in what needs to be done.
  - o Give clear timescales.
  - o Set expectations around the desired outcome.
  - o Explain how you see this being achieved.
  - o Agree regular checkpoints.
- Don't:
  - o Allow individual to undertake a task unless you are able to provide the time to give clear directions.

2 Not willing and not able – Guiding style.

- Do:
  - o Explain to team members the value of the task to the overall objectives.
  - o Provide clear direction in what needs to be done.
  - o Give clear timescales.
  - o Set expectations around the desired outcome.
  - o Guide through the stages of the task.
  - o Encourage the team to try new tasks or a new approach.
  - o Offer support and establish what this looks like.
  - o Agree regular checkpoints.
- Don't:
  - o Leave them to get on with it.
  - o Delegate responsibility.

3 Not willing and yet able – Supportive style.

- Do:
  - o Explain to the team the value of the task to the overall objectives.
  - o Jointly establish what needs to be done.
  - o Jointly agree clear timescales.
  - o Ask the team to talk through how they will approach and progress with the task.
  - o Encourage them to have a go!
  - o Explore their fears or reasons for being hesitant to approach the task.
  - o Understand how they can increase their commitment to what they are being asked to do.
  - o Point out your confidence in their ability.
  - o Establish what support they need, and from whom.
- Don't:
  - o Tell them what to do!
  - o Be prescriptive.

4 Willing and able – Delegation and Coaching style.

- Do:
  - o Allow individual to scope the task and expectations of the outcome.
  - o Allow them to set realistic, challenging timescales.
  - o Retain accountability.
  - o Agree regular checkpoints to review performance.
  - o Make sure the individual is being stretched.

Your leadership style

In order to bring this to life, think of an example of one of your own members of staff. Plot where their willingness and ability is in relation to a task that you have given them. Consider the leadership style that you adopted in this circumstance and whether this was most appropriate to this person.

Next time you sit down with an individual to take on a new task or to review how they are progressing, think about their willingness and ability and adapt your leadership style to achieve their best performance.

Even if you are asking one of your most competent people to undertake a new activity, always assess where they are and what they need from you.

Activities to undertake with your team

I suggest that you explain the two models that I have outlined in this chapter to your team.

You can use the followers' behaviour model (Figure 10) when discussing performance issues with your team by asking individuals to assess where they think they are on the model. If you find that they move between the boxes, seek to understand what triggers these changes and challenge them to think of what they need to do to make sure they are in the High Performers box.

Likewise you can discuss the ability and willingness model with your team. Ask individuals to identify where they are in the model when they are given a task. This will help you to adapt your style to meet their needs.

Summary

In this chapter I have outlined the support and challenge model of leadership and the consequent behaviours that this can encourage in followers. I have also outlined the leadership adaptability model, which it is useful to consider in relation to followers' ability and willingness to undertake a task.

In order to bring the points in this chapter to life, here are some questions to ask yourself:

- What one thing can you do to adopt a more supportive and challenging climate?
- What are the predominant behaviours that you view in your team? How can you ensure that you encourage high performance?
- What do you need to consider when giving a task to a team member?
- Looking at the leadership adaptability model, what style do you find it easiest to use? And most difficult?
- What actions can you take to ensure that you do adapt your style to the individual, the task and the situation?

Suggested answers

- Scenario 1
  - I tend to leave my team to their own devices.

Abdicator

  - I seek to maintain a steady pace of work with my team.

Coach

- o I drive my team hard to achieve their goals.

Taskmaster

- o I am supportive of my team.

Counsellor

- Scenario 2
  - o I avoid conflict at all cost.

Abdicator

- o I try to avoid conflict, but if it occurs I try to smooth things over in a friendly way.

Counsellor

- o When there is conflict I defend my position with counter-arguments.

Taskmaster

- o When there is conflict I keep calm and try to develop a joint solution.

Coach

- Scenario 3
  - o My style could be described as counselling.

Counsellor

- o My style could be described as defensive.

Taskmaster

- o My style could be described as *laissez-faire*.

Abdicator

- o My style could be described as consultative.

Coach

- Scenario 4
  - I rarely give feedback on others' performance.

Abdicator

  - I find it easy to give motivational feedback.

Counsellor

  - I tell people how they can improve.

Taskmaster

  - My feedback is a balance of motivational and developmental advice.

Coach

- Scenario 5
  - I place high value on maintaining good relations.

Counsellor

  - I tend to do my own thing.

Abdicator

  - I search for workable solutions.

Coach

  - I tend to impose my decisions.

Taskmaster

- Scenario 6
  - I use humour to maintain friendly situations or when there is disagreement, to shift things away from serious discussion.

Counsellor

o My humour can be seen by others as rather pointless.

Abdicator

o My humour is hard-hitting.

Taskmaster

o My humour fits the situation and I retain a sense of humour even under pressure.

Coach

CHAPTER 3: LEADING YOURSELF

In this chapter I outline:

- Why it is important that you increase your self-awareness to become a better leader
- Techniques you can use to increase your self-awareness
- A self-assessment leadership model.

Increasing your self-awareness as a leader

It is commonly acknowledged that there are three basic ways to become a leader:

- Some people demonstrate extraordinary leadership qualities in a crisis or important event, which causes them to rise to the occasion.
- Some people are born with natural personality traits that lead them into leadership roles.
- Some people can learn leadership skills and choose to become leaders. I am sure that this applies to you and it is the principle on which this book is based.

In order to learn to be a leader, therefore, you need to be conscious of who you are, of how others perceive you and of what your strengths and development areas are.

As we saw in Chapter 1, when followers decide whether or not they are willing to be led by you, they make decisions based on your behaviours, as well as on how you *are*. The basis of good leadership in your team members' eyes is how you are (being), what your beliefs are and what your character is like, for example; what you know (knowing), your skills, knowledge and experience, for example; and what you do (doing), such as setting direction, inspiring others and following through.

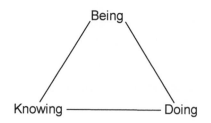

Figure 12: Being, knowing, doing

So what do you know about yourself? How comfortable are you with what you stand for? What aspects of your leadership do you need to develop?

Using feedback from others

Within your organisation, you probably have methods open to you to help gather feedback from others on what they perceive to be your strengths and your areas for development. This could be feedback you have received from customers and colleagues, from your manager and from team members. It could be part of performance reviews, one-to-one discussions or a more formal 360° feedback process. You can also ask friends and family for their feedback.

Self-assessment using the leadership compass

One way of assessing who you are, what are your strengths and development areas are as a leader, is to use the leadership compass as an assessment tool.

Recent research has illustrated that the most important qualities of the effective leader are not the disconnected set of skills or knowledge that they possess. Rather, they relate to four intelligences: business intelligence (BQ), political intelligence (PQ), spiritual intelligence (SQ) and emotional intelligence (EQ). In essence, these represent the following:

- Business intelligence: the foresight to envision the future and the drive to move the business forward.

- Spiritual intelligence: knowing who you are, self-belief and sense of purpose. Creativity is a subset of this intelligence.

- Political intelligence: knowing the bases of power, knowing who to influence and how.

- Emotional intelligence: recognising others' feelings, building strong trusting relationships.

Depicted as four points of a compass, these intelligences help leaders to navigate well in their roles.

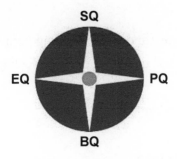

Figure 13: The leadership compass

Like the four points of a compass, they have equal weight. If the leader is missing one or more of the intelligences, the compass becomes unbalanced and unreliable, the pathway becomes unclear.

Business intelligence involves:

- Business expertise or competence.
- Thinking ahead strategically.
- Listening to and anticipating customer demands.
- Planning to meet customer demands.
- Developing customer-driven offerings and solutions.
- Taking opportunities to improve services to the customer.

Leaders with business intelligence anticipate changing customer demands. They translate this knowledge into service offers and operational processes that deliver successfully to the customer. They are proactive in managing customer expectations and ensure that their businesses are customer-friendly.

Emotional intelligence is the ability to recognise one's own and others' emotions; the impact that these emotions have is critical. Behaviours which demonstrate emotional intelligence include:

- Being self-aware and understanding your own feelings.
- Recognising and understanding the feelings of others.
- Listening.
- Being open and empathic.
- Sharing feelings.
- Appreciating others.

Emotions and feelings play a much bigger role in change than is sometimes recognised in a rationally oriented management world.

Spiritual intelligence is sometimes described as having an understanding of one's values and contribution in life, as knowing:

- Your life purpose.
- Your personal goals and contribution.
- The value you bring to 'the world'.

Political intelligence, as I define it, involves:

- Being aware of power bases.
- Understanding sources of power.
- Recognising levers of influence during change.
- Developing strategies for influence.
- Gaining buy-in from stakeholders.

PQ, BQ, SQ and EQ add up to the qualities that leaders need in order to drive high performance at work:

- Business intelligence provides the vision and strategy for the future, the sound business case for moving forward, the credible drive and inspiration to others.
- Spiritual intelligence provides the sense of purpose and the self-belief that leaders need.
- Emotional intelligence engenders positive relationships; it provides nurturing qualities and creates positive team spirit.
- Political intelligence promotes understanding of stakeholders' issues and concerns, of networking and of why buy-in is necessary to change.

Identify your strengths

It is probable that we have refined one or two of the intelligences rather more than others and that you feel comfortable using these preferred or favoured ones. However, effective leaders need to have high levels of intelligence in all four areas. Use the following assessment to identify your leadership strengths and areas for development.

Look at the descriptors in the four sections below. Put a tick beside the ones that best describe you. The results will help you to start to assess your leanings on the leadership compass, and your strengths. In this context there are no rights and wrongs, and it works best if you give your first reactions rather than ponder for a long time over each word.

Quick
Confident
Persuasive
Forceful
Competitive
Strong-willed
Inspiring
Action-oriented
Determined

Opinionated
Total ticks section 1
Precise
Deliberate
Economical
Analytical
Practical
Comfortable with details
Questioning
Objective
Informative
Authoritative
Total ticks section 2
Trusting
Supporting
Responsive
Helpful
Receptive
Encouraging

Empathetic
Sharing
Relaxed
Warm
Total ticks section 3
Enthusiastic
Creative
Imaginative
Persuasive
Dynamic
Adaptable
Animated
Experimental
'Sparky'
Inspired
Total ticks section 4

Table 2: Leadership compass assessment

Now look at the box or boxes with the highest number of ticks and the second-highest number of ticks.

Section 1 relates to **action-oriented** behaviour – if you scored the highest or second highest in this area your BQ and PQ are likely to be more developed than your EQ and SQ. The rationale is that your imperative for action may override concerns for individuals or perhaps block out wider, longer-term reflection and inner sense of purpose.

Section 2 relates to **order-oriented** behaviour – if you scored the highest or second highest in this area your PQ and BQ may be more developed than your EQ and SQ. A high score here suggests a potential rigidity in times of change, which will not easily allow new data into your mindset.

Section 3 relates to **nurture-oriented** behaviour – if you scored the highest or second highest in this area your EQ and SQ may be more developed than your BQ and PQ. A relatively high score implies a concern for people which can sometimes dominate the need to take objective business decisions or to take decisions to win over power bases and critical enemies.

Section 4 relates to **creative-oriented** behaviour – if you scored the highest or second highest in this area your SQ and EQ may be more developed than your BQ and PQ. A highly creative approach is not always suited to the realities of business and you may feel impatient with those who block fresh ideas. You may certainly be driven by your own sense of mission.

If you have the same score in two or three areas, look at the area or areas where you have the lowest scores. This is where you need to develop.

Below is a summary of the potential outcomes of your self-assessment.

Order	Action
PQ and BQ	BQ and PQ
Likely to project-manage with a clear idea of use of resources.	Proactive, short-term focus.
Weighs up people and business criteria objectively.	Likely to be impatient, for example if change gets blocked.
Finds handling known parameters more comfortable than unknown.	Provides a strong sense of urgency.
Nurture	**Creativity**
EQ and SQ	SQ and EQ
Concerned to bring others with them. Strong on engaging others.	Enjoys work which is new and different.
May be reluctant to take decisions which adversely affect others.	May find routine implementation dull.
Takes a visible ethical stance.	Has clear, confident stance on their abilities and ideas.

Figure 14: Order, action, nurture, creativity

Activity to undertake with your team

As a means of checking if your own perception of yourself is correct, ask someone in your team who knows you well to undertake the same assessment, then compare scores.

Identifying leadership potential

We have the potential to use all points of the leadership compass, but the chances are that you are well practised in using the areas at work where you scored highest. The challenge is to raise your comfort levels with the points of the compass where you scored lowest. You can do this by learning skills, attitudes and approaches that I outline in this book. You can also read Cook, Macaulay and Coldicott's *Effective Change Management* for more details on BQ, SQ, EQ and PQ.

Summary

The starting point for developing your leadership skills is to create awareness of your strengths and development areas in terms of leadership. You can do this by asking others formally or informally for feedback. You can also use the leadership compass as the starting point for increasing your self-awareness.

Here are some questions to ask of yourself and others:

- What are my skills and qualities as a business leader? How good am I at setting direction, goals and strategy for the future?
- How able am I to read the political situation and influence others effectively?
- What are my relationships with others like? How empathic am I to others' needs?
- What are my personal values? How do they act as guiding principles for me as a leader?

CHAPTER 4: LEADING THE BUSINESS

In this chapter I focus on:

- How effective leaders develop a vision for their department.
- How to set departmental objectives and strategy.
- The importance of communicating clearly to team members the vision, goals and strategy.

People want to be guided by those they respect and who have a clear sense of direction. You can provide a sense of direction as a leader by conveying a strong vision of the future, setting clear objectives and a strategy to achieve the vision that is shared by all of your team.

According to a study by the global management consultancy Hay Group, trust and confidence in leadership is the single most reliable predictor of employee satisfaction in an organisation. They identified that leaders need to communicate effectively in three key areas:

- Helping team members understand the vision and business strategy of the department and the organisation.
- Making clear how team members contribute to achieving key business objectives.
- Providing ongoing information about how the department and business is doing in relation to its key objectives.

Developing a vision for the IT department

As Henry Kissinger said, 'If you do not know where you are going, every road will get you nowhere'.

Developing a team vision creates a sense of purpose for your team, so that all of you know what the team is aiming for and aspiring to in the future. Creating a team vision helps people identify the role they play as individuals in achieving team goals.

Here is a process that you can work though in order to create a vision of the future with your team. I suggest that this is done collectively, so that you have a shared sense of where you are heading. The process requires you to hold a team meeting to think of current team successes, of what you want in the future and of how to bridge the gap between these.

The first activity that I suggest you undertake with your team is to brainstorm and record a selection of successes that you have generated as a team. Everyone should have an opportunity to voice their two key successes.

Collectively pull together the top two successes from each member of the team. Remember to celebrate the successes that you have had and to thank team members for their efforts.

Now ask the team to imagine a time in the future where you as a team are performing at 100% for your people and your customers, with the right level of organisational support. Ask the team, 'what will it be like for us, and for our customers?'

Ask everyone to take five minutes to think alone and capture some thoughts about this. They can do this by jotting down their thoughts on a piece of paper or a flipchart – they can even draw a picture to represent what it would be like.

To help them do this, ask team members to close their eyes and to imagine the place where they do their best thinking. This may be lying in bed, or on the sofa, or sat at their desk. They need to visualise themselves there.

Encourage the whole group to develop a vision that feels right both intellectually and emotionally for them individually.

Use the following questions as prompts:

- Who are our customers?
- How would our new customers feel?
- What difference would existing customers notice?
- What would the atmosphere be like in our workplace?
- What will we be doing differently?
- What would success look, feel and sound like?
- What do we need to continue doing and what do we need to start doing?

When everyone has had a few minutes of individual thinking, ask the team members to explain their responses to the whole group. Ensure that everyone is allowed some airtime. Write down the key themes from each person's vision on a flipchart. When all ideas have been captured, summarise the key themes and language. Encourage the team to create a vision statement that everyone is happy to call their vision.

Test it against these criteria: inspiring, motivational, achievable and memorable. If it is all these things, it is likely to be a compelling team vision.

Setting departmental goals and strategy

When you have created a team vision, you will need to look with the team at how you bridge the gap between where you are now and where you want to be – your vision. In order to arrive at your vision as a team, it is useful to set some goals for achieving the vision and a strategy for how you will work towards achieving the goals.

One technique to help you set departmental goals and strategy is to undertake a review with your team of how you work. Investigate the following areas with your team:

- customer feedback
- team structure and staffing levels
- team skills and development areas
- systems and processes
- financial constraints.

Customer feedback

Use your feedback to help you assess how your department is currently perceived by your customers. If you do not seek feedback from customers on at least a quarterly basis, consider how you could do this, as it is best practice.

Use the feedback that you receive to help identify your strengths and areas for improvement.

Think about how well you demonstrate customer orientation to your team. Below are some activities and questions to consider.

Honestly rate customer contact against your other departmental priorities. How truly important is this to you?
When did you last speak to a customer? Did you implement what you learned?
How do you know what problems your people encounter when dealing with customers? When did you last update this knowledge?
What is the gap between your department's intended service and how you really deal with the customer?
Have you reviewed your organisational structure specifically for its customer orientation? Where do customer-facing employees sit in the hierarchy?
What messages does your leadership style send to the customer and to the rest of the organisation?

What feedback do you have to support this?
How do you support and strengthen your staff's abilities to deal successfully with customers?
Do you address difficult issues which impede customer service?
Are the systems you operate likely to encourage customer satisfaction?
Are reward and motivation systems linked correctly to delivering customer satisfaction?

Table 3: Leadership considerations around the customer

Team structure and staffing levels

Look at how your team is currently structured and the roles and responsibilities of each member of your team. Given your customer requirements, review whether you have the right structure and numbers of staff to meet their needs. Consider how customer needs will change in the forthcoming year and what this means for your team structure.

Team skills and development areas

Undertake a review of the skills set of your team. Do your team have the necessary knowledge, ability and experience to fulfil future customer requirements? Where are the skills gaps? What development opportunities are there for the team going forward?

Systems and processes

How effective are your departmental systems and processes? Are they fit for purpose? Consider where there are bottlenecks, or where systems and processes can be updated. What are other organisations, or parts of your own organisation, doing that you can learn from?

Financial constraints

What is your departmental budget? How well do you manage your team finances? Consider how your financial constraints are likely to change in the next twelve months.

As a result of the review that you undertake with your team, you should be able to agree a set of departmental objectives. Do ensure that these relate to your organisation's objectives and strategy.

Consider how your departmental objectives relate to your customers, to your people, to learning and development, to budgets and to processes and systems.

Ensure that you agree the objectives with your team, and that you set specific timescales and measures for their success. It is helpful also to agree when and how these will be reviewed.

Having established the vision and goals of the IT department, together with measures of success, the next step is to develop a strategy for achieving these.

Communication

The vision, goals and strategy of your team will only come to life if they are constantly communicated and reviewed.

Several things distinguish leaders who successfully communicate their vision and strategic goals to employees. These are:

- They use a variety of different communications media to get their message across in an interactive way.
- They are approachable.
- They constantly reinforce the message.

Take a sheet of paper and list all the methods there are to communicate with your team. These can be as conventional as the intranet, team meetings, newsletters, message boards, emails and personal voice messages. Although one-to-one communication is important, there are a myriad of media that you can use to inform employees of key goals and of how these relate to individual jobs.

Here is a checklist to assess your own performance in informing employees in a motivating way about the department's vision and strategic objectives.

Criteria	In place	Not applicable	Needs to be actioned or addressed
My department has a clear vision of the future			
Our departmental vision is well communicated across the team			
I can describe the organisational vision in a motivational way			
Our team has a clear set of goals			
These goals are known and understood by team members			
I remind team members at least once every six			

months about the department's vision and goals			
I use a variety of methods to communicate our vision, goals and strategy			

Table 4: Communications checklist

Summary

In order to provide effective leadership of the business, I suggest that you work with your team to develop a vision for the IT department, that you set clear departmental objectives and strategy, and that you clearly communicate and review these with your team.

Here are some questions to ask yourself and members of your team:

- How often do you review your departmental objectives with your team? Is this an appropriate time period?
- How well do you currently communicate your departmental vision? How do you know this?
- What do you and your team think would be better ways of reminding everyone about the goals of the department?

- How often do you communicate the team's progress relative to the goals? What else can you do in this respect?

CHAPTER 5: LEADING OTHERS

In this chapter I outline:

- The importance of personal presence and impact in leading others.
- The importance of emotional intelligence.
- How to influence others effectively.

Personal presence and impact

In order to bring others with you as a leader, you need to be able to influence effectively. Being aware of your own style of communication and preferences is a first step.

Typically, people have a preference for one of four basic styles of communication. At times they may use a combination of two styles. These styles are:

- Direct:
  o taking charge
  o communicating directly
  o assertive
  o focused on the big picture.
- Engaging:
  o persuasive
  o energetic
  o enthusiastic
  o spontaneous.
- Systematic:

- o detailed, focused
- o analytical
- o methodical
- o thorough.
- Cohesive:
  - o considerate
  - o actively listening
  - o collaborative
  - o patient.

Look at the following words and allocate a total of 20 points to this list. The points you allocate should reflect how much you feel each word represents you.

	Your points allocation
taking charge	
communicating directly	
assertive	
focused on the big picture	
persuasive	
energetic	
enthusiastic	
spontaneous	
detailed, focused	

analytical	
methodical	
thorough	
considerate	
actively listening	
collaborative	
patient	

Table 5: Personality styles

Now look at where you have scored your points. Count how many points are in each category.

- Direct:
  - taking charge
  - communicating directly
  - assertive
  - focused on the big picture.
- Engaging:
  - persuasive
  - energetic
  - enthusiastic
  - spontaneous.
- Systematic:
  - detailed, focused
  - analytical

- o methodical
- o thorough.
- Cohesive:
  - o considerate
  - o actively listening
  - o collaborative
  - o patient.

Your personality style is shown by the category or categories in which you have scored highest.

The challenge for leaders is to adapt their style to the target audience. People who are engaging, for instance, may get impatient and 'switch off' if they are presented material in a very systematic manner. Consider the personality preferences of several members of your team, for example. How different are they from your own? What might you need to do to modify your communication style in order to have a more positive impact with these people?

Emotional intelligence

Recognising your own style and adapting it to the needs of others is an example of emotional intelligence (EQ).

EQ is defined by Daniel Goleman, author of *Working with Emotional Intelligence*, as 'the capacity for recognising our feelings and those of others, for motivating ourselves and for managing emotions well in ourselves and in our relationships'.

There are four aspects of EQ:

- self-awareness

- self-management
- awareness of others
- relating to others.

In order to understand the characteristics of each of these four areas, here is a short assessment for you to complete. Look at the answers at the end of the chapter to check if your responses are correct.

Self-awareness

- Which of the following *do* characterise emotional self-awareness?
  - o I know what motivates me.
  - o I know when I am angry, sad, happy or frightened.
  - o Occasionally I am not aware of the impact my behaviour has on others.
  - o I know what skills I am competent in.
  - o I am aware of situations that cause me to think negatively.
  - o I am confident in myself.
  - o Sometimes I do not know why I act the way I do.

Self-management

- Which of the following *do not* characterise emotional self-management?
  - o My anger tends to be explosive.
  - o I take setbacks in my stride.
  - o If something goes wrong at the start of the day, I know the rest of the day will be bad too.

o I set myself achievable goals.

o I am adaptable.

o I sometimes lack initiative and drive.

o I use positive 'self-talk' to help me achieve my goals.

Awareness of others

- Which of the following behaviours *do* characterise emotional awareness of others?

  o I recognise others when they have done a good job.

  o I am sensitive to my team members' needs.

  o I know when someone says something that they do not really mean.

  o I sense when others are not happy.

  o I do not know what makes my team tick.

  o I know when to contribute to a conversation and when to stay silent.

  o I know what is important to the people with whom I work.

Relating to others

- Which of the following *do not* characterise emotional relating to others?

  o I can chat with some people in the team on a friendly basis.

  o I find it easy to develop others' potential.

  o Helping others through change is not always easy.

  o I find it difficult sometimes to influence others to my way of thinking.

o I build trust with my customers and my team.
o If someone is having a hard time, I am supportive of them.
o Sometimes I find it easier to deal with facts than with feelings.

By being aware of yourself as a leader, by managing your emotions and being aware of others, you are able to build strong relationships. Having high levels of emotional intelligence also means that you are more likely to be able to influence others effectively.

How to influence others effectively

Since one definition of leadership is influencing others to achieve organisational goals, your ability as a leader is very much dependent on how well you influence others.

What do I mean by the term 'influence'? Day to day we find ourselves in a variety of situations where, as leaders, we need to bring others round to our way of thinking, to do something for us or to approach something in a certain way. Given that the people we interact with day to day are likely to be the people we continue to deal with, we need to be able to influence others in a way that demonstrates respect for them. In simple terms, this means that we need to be able to convince them whilst maintaining rapport and a long-term relationship with them.

Most of us have good intentions in what we do as leaders, whether it is developing rapport with someone or carrying out a task. However, on occasions it becomes apparent that the result of our behaviour has not had the impact we intended.

When we or others describe what has happened, we are likely to refer to the type of words used, the tone of voice and the body language. This is the way in which we communicate.

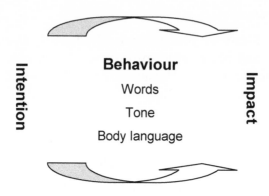

Intention

Behaviour

Words

Tone

Body language

Impact

Figure 15: Intention versus impact

To have the impact we desire, whether putting forward a point of view or delivering a presentation, our words, tone and body language need to be congruent. That is, they need to work in harmony.

If our impact proves to have been different from what we intended, we are likely to find that our actions and words were not congruent, thereby creating misunderstanding in others. Other people may see us as non-assertive, or as adopting either an aggressive or a passive style of communication. This can result in them losing respect for us as leaders.

Most people can describe intuitively the impact that the behaviour of others has had on them. Many of us have described, or heard others describe, the influence the behaviour of others has. For example,

- 'He really **pushes** people around.'
- 'She really puts her **points across well**.'
- 'I can really **relate** to him.'

The push/pull model of influence

One model of influence that you will find useful explores the use of energy, which is used differently depending on whether we are using **push** or **pull** behaviour:

- Energy is used from within to **push** others in order to influence them.
- Energy is used from others to **pull** them in order to influence them.

The model introduces different influence behaviours, which enable us to reach a result or outcome that is agreeable to both parties. The words that are used as part of the model, as well as the tone and the body language, need to be congruent. This then increases our ability to influence others and communicate our willingness to be influenced.

Push behaviours relate to when you state views and opinions, expectations, wants and needs. They also relate to when you offer incentives, state the consequences or express how you feel. Push statements often start with 'I', such as 'I want', 'I need' or 'I expect'. The impact of push behaviours is to drive people to change.

Pull behaviours, however, involve asking questions to solicit views, ideas and information from others, and encouraging participation in discussion. They also involve active listening, building common ground with others and being open to others' ideas. Here the language used is much more that of 'you' and 'we'. Pull behaviours signal to the other person that you are more prepared to learn and possibly change.

Push and pull behaviours can be used to influence guests and colleagues in a positive way. However, in practice you may find that some of the behaviours are less natural to you than others and need to be practised so that they become learned.

Look at the list below, and distinguish between push behaviours that encourage other people to do things differently and pull behaviours which signal that you are willing to change. Identify whether the statements that follow are examples of push or pull techniques.

Statement	Push or pull behaviour?
'In my opinion we need to ...'	
'So what you're saying is ...'	
'I need to know when you need it by.'	
'How did this happen?'	
'You're right, we did make an error there.'	
'If you do that, I'd be prepared to ...'	
'I agree, that's a good idea.'	

'I believe that's the best way because ...'	
'So, we all agree that we should ...'	
'You don't sound as though you are convinced.'	
'What do you think we should do next?'	
'I want you to be responsible for timekeeping.'	
'Right now I'm feeling as though we're not getting anywhere.'	
'I feel really pleased about what we have achieved so far.'	
'I am quite good at this type of activity.'	
'I suggest we do this first.'	
'If you do that we will run out of time.'	

Table 6: Push and pull behaviours

If you are having difficulty influencing others effectively, ask yourself which is your predominant style of influence: is it push or is it pull? What is the balance of your use of each style?

If you use more a push style of communication you may be seen by others as aggressive or 'pushy'. If you use more pull than push, your influencing style may be seen by others as too docile and passive. The key is to ensure that on the whole you use a balance between the two styles in order to influence effectively and bring people with you.

Activities to undertake with your team

Ask your team to describe your style of influence. Discuss with them the impact of the way that you communicate. Seek feedback from colleagues on what you can do to lead others better in an assertive fashion.

Summary

In this chapter I have discussed the need to be aware of your personal presence and impact in leading others. I have also outlined the four aspects of emotional intelligence, and how these underpin the ability to influence effectively. Finally, I have discussed the push/pull model of influence, which, if applied in equal measures, can ensure a positive outcome and strong working relationships.

Here are some questions to ask of yourself:

- Which personality styles best describe you? What are the implications for you of these styles?
- On a scale of 1 to 10, where 10 = excellent, how do you rate your:
  o Self-awareness?
  o Self-management?
  o Awareness of others?

o Ability to relate to others?

- What can you improve?

- Which aspects of push and pull do you need to focus on more in order to achieve a successful outcome?

Suggested answers

The suggested answers are highlighted in **bold**:

Self-awareness

- Which of the following *do* characterise emotional self-awareness?
  o **I know what motivates me.**
  o **I know when I am angry, sad, happy or frightened.**
  o Occasionally I am not aware of the impact my behaviour has on others.
  o I know what skills I am competent in.
  o **I am aware of situations that cause me to think negatively.**
  o **I am confident in myself.**
  o Sometimes I do not know why I act the way I do.

Self-management

- Which of the following *do not* characterise emotional self-management?
  o **My anger tends to be explosive.**
  o I take setbacks in my stride.

o **If something goes wrong at the start of the day, I know the rest of the day will be bad too.**

o I set myself achievable goals.

o I am adaptable.

o **I sometimes lack initiative and drive.**

o I use positive 'self-talk' to help me achieve my goals.

Awareness of others

* Which of the following behaviours *do* characterise emotional awareness of others?

  o **I recognise others when they have done a good job.**

  o **I am sensitive to my team members' needs.**

  o **I know when someone says something that they do not really mean.**

  o **I sense when others are not happy.**

  o I do not know what makes my team tick.

  o **I know when to contribute to a conversation and when to stay silent.**

  o **I know what is important to the people with whom I work.**

Relating to others

* Which of the following *do not* characterise emotional relating to others?

  o **I can chat with some people in the team on a friendly basis.**

  o I find it easy to develop others' potential.

  o **Helping others through change is not always easy.**

o **I find it difficult sometimes to influence others to my way of thinking.**

o I build trust with my customers and my team.

o If someone is having a hard time, I am supportive of them.

o **Sometimes I find it easier to deal with facts than with feelings.**

Statement	Push or pull behaviour?
'In my opinion we need to ...'	Push – stating views and opinions
'So what you're saying is ...'	Pull – active listening
'I need to know when you need it by.'	Push – stating what I want
'How did this happen?'	Pull - questioning
'You're right, we did make an error there.'	Pull – being open
'If you do that, I'd be prepared to ...'	Push – stating incentives and consequences
'I agree, that's a good idea.'	Pull – building common ground
'I believe that's the best way because ...'	Push – stating views and opinions

'So, we all agree that we should ...'	Pull – building common ground
'You don't sound as though you are convinced.'	Pull – active listening
'What do you think we should do next?'	Pull – questioning
'I want you to be responsible for timekeeping.'	Push – stating what I want
'Right now I'm feeling as though we're not getting anywhere.'	Push – disclosing feelings
'I feel really pleased about what we have achieved so far.'	Push – disclosing feelings
'I am quite good at this type of activity.'	Pull – being open
'I suggest we do this first.'	Push – stating views and opinions
'If you do that we will run out of time.'	Push – stating incentives and consequences

Table 7: Push and pull behaviours – suggested answers

CHAPTER 6: EMPOWERING OTHERS

In this chapter I outline:

- How effective leadership encourages empowerment.
- The four levels of empowerment.
- How to delegate effectively.

Encouraging empowerment

This chapter looks at how you can empower people and, in doing so, challenge and encourage them to take responsibility and release their potential. Empowerment involves the devolvement of decision making to team members. The benefits of empowerment include:

- Greater decision making for individuals.
- More sense of ownership and responsibility.
- Higher levels of customer satisfaction as staff are given the power to make decisions to increase customer loyalty.

Traditionally, many organisational departments, including IT, tend to adopt a command-and-control type of leadership. This means that many team members are not encouraged to make decisions without referring to the leader. Removing some of these barriers enables people to create an environment that is motivational and produces excellent results. People are likely to go the extra mile when they feel responsible for their own actions. An empowered environment also encourages effective processes, procedures and personal action.

We are all managed and led by someone and we all manage and lead others, yet often we are so engrossed in the latter task that we do not take time out to consider what sort of environment we are creating for our people.

So, how do you create an environment where people are empowered?

Think of an occasion when you have received work or a specific output from one of your team that made you believe that the individual felt empowered. Think back and consider what it was that you did as a leader that provoked the individual to act in that way. What was the impact of your behaviour?

So, can you empower someone? My belief is that you can only create the environment in which people feel empowered and able to make decisions for themselves – you cannot take those decisions for them. Our behaviours as leaders will either encourage or discourage people's taking the initiative. This is at the heart of empowerment – you cannot give it over on a plate, wrap it up like a present – it is something you have to encourage in your environment so that people feel they want to take it.

The four levels of empowerment

So, how do you create the right environment?

This is about being very clear where people can take decisions without referring to you and where they need to ask permission.

There are four levels of empowerment that exist:

1 Stop – no permission.

2 Ask, then do.

3 Do, then let me know.

4 Do.

In order to create an environment that allows others to feel empowered, you need to be very clear about which elements of work that your team undertakes belong in which of the four levels. This gives you a framework for initiative and innovation.

Level 1: Stop – no permission. This is total disempowerment. Some areas of work are necessarily off-limits, such as safety, legalities and security. People need to know that they are not allowed to do certain things or only allowed to do them in a prescribed way, the way you have to drive on the left in the UK, for example. Your organisation will have policies and procedures that outline these. The message you give with 'Stop – no permission' is 'I need you to do it like this'.

Level 2: Ask, then do. This is where people are still largely disempowered. They have to ask and get permission before they can go ahead. For example, using the driving analogy, you need to get a driving licence and be 17 years old before you can drive a car on the road in the UK. A work example might be requesting to work overtime to meet a tight deadline.

Level 3: Do, then let me know. This is where people are basically empowered. They can make their own decisions but need to let you know what they have done. For example, an IT team member in technical support may loan someone a laptop if theirs needs mending. Yet the right people still need to be notified that this has been done.

Level 4: Do. This represents total empowerment and complete freedom of action. For example, a member of staff may take ownership of a customer complaint and go out of their way to resolve it. It may not be necessary to ask you about this or even to let you know.

The key to creating an empowering climate is to be clear about your expectations of others. If I asked your team, would they all say they were crystal clear on what your expectations are and on the boundaries and parameters you had set for them in their day-to-day tasks?

Assess which level of empowerment you use most in your team

Look back over the past week and the work that you have allocated to your team members. Complete the following assessment sheet to identify which level of empowerment you used most frequently.

For each team member, list the tasks that you allocated and what level of empowerment you granted them to do the task						
Team member (insert name)						
1. Stop – no permission						
2. Ask, then do						

3. Do, then let me know						
4. Do						

Table 8: Assessment of level of empowerment

When you have completed the assessment, look at the levels of empowerment for each task. For each task, ask yourself: is this appropriate? What could you have done to encourage a higher level of empowerment?

Look at the levels that you use most overall. Again, ask yourself: is this appropriate? What would need to change for you to increase the levels of empowerment in your department?

Effective delegation

The more competent and confident a person is in doing a task, the more opportunity there is to empower them. As a leader, you need to consider the competence and confidence of your people and how willing they are to take responsibility.

As well as being clear about the level of empowerment to act that team members have, achieving an empowered team is created through effective delegation.

Delegation saves us time as leaders. It encourages the personal development of individuals in our team and encourages empowerment. Yet there are many reasons why leaders do not delegate. Do any of these sound familiar?

- 'I can do it more quickly myself.'

- 'It's too risky – I can't afford mistakes.'
- 'I'm responsible, so I must keep control.'
- 'I like doing this work myself.'
- 'I'm too busy. It would take me too long to explain what they would have to do.'
- 'I might not be there to help if they get into difficulties.'
- 'I'm not sure if they'll be able to cope.'
- 'They might think I'm offloading my work onto them.'
- 'It's difficult to find time to develop my staff.'
- 'I'll get the blame if the work is late or substandard.'
- 'I need to be involved because I should know what's going on in my department.'

The problem is that if you do not let go, you always end up either doing the work yourself or having a team who are totally reliant on you for decisions. Delegation does take time initially, but in the long run it saves you time.

When delegating a task,

- Think about the individual who you want to delegate to – are they the right person and is it right for them?
- Are they willing and able?
- Do they have the skills and knowledge to undertake the task? Ensure that you look at each task individually; for example, it is often easy to think that if someone has a great way of speaking to customers on the phone, they can deal with all telephone calls, but this may not be the best solution.
- Think about the experience they have had and what further training or support they will need.

- Consider whether the role or task will stretch the person and check that they want the stretch.
- Think what support is needed – how can this be given and by whom?
- Be clear what are the timescales for the work.
- Ensure that you know what your expectations around the work are.

It is important, when you delegate, that you communicate:

- The desired result.
- Guidelines and boundaries, and any principles, policies and procedures that are essential to getting the result.
- The scope of the work, and any resources required.
- The key people they need to involve.
- Timescales and budget, if applicable.

Once you have delegated the task, ensure that you offer support and guidance, depending upon the individual's willingness and ability. It is fine to observe the individual undertaking the task, but don't monitor them or interfere. This is not empowerment. Likewise, don't abdicate. This is not empowerment either.

After completion of the task, ensure that you:

- Provide feedback which is timely and objective.
- Ask the individual to review how it went and what they could have done differently. Is this something they would like to do more of?
- Who can they pass their knowledge on to, effectively delegating to others?
- Is there a better way of undertaking the task?

- Can they share their experience with others?

Activities to undertake with your team

Share with your team the four levels of empowerment. Discuss with them their perceptions of which level you use most when you ask them to undertake a task. Have an open discussion around whether this is appropriate. Ask them what more you can do to encourage an empowering climate in the team.

Summary

In this chapter I have outlined how effective leadership encourages empowerment and the four levels of empowerment. I have also provided you with tips on how to delegate effectively.

Here are some questions to ask yourself, having read this chapter:

- What can you do to create a more empowered environment in your team?

- What support, training or coaching do your team need to feel more empowered?

- What do you need to do to ensure that you delegate effectively?

- What do you need to tell yourself to ensure that you don't undertake activities yourself that you could delegate to others?

CHAPTER 7: ACTION PLANNING

In this chapter I outline how to:

- Recognise your strengths as a leader.
- Prepare a personal development plan to increase your leadership capability.

Recognising your strengths

Great leaders are those who are able to display a positive, but realistic, attitude towards themselves without being arrogant. They are confident in their abilities and know where their strengths lie. In doing so,

- They are more willing to admit when things go wrong, so there is an opportunity to fix them.
- The style they use allows for consideration of others' viewpoints; they also have the ability to express their own.
- They are more likely to take a risk and manage what comes out of it.
- They are more likely to believe that they can achieve the desired outcome.
- They are more willing to seek the views of others because they do not believe that they must, or could, have the right answer all the time.

Part of being an effective leader, therefore, is having knowledge of, and confidence in, one's own key strengths. One of the reasons we may suffer from lack of confidence as a leader is because we allow too many negative thoughts to invade our minds. This in turn can create feelings of failure and rejection as a leader.

As you have been reading this book, and based on the feedback you have received from others in the past year or so, you have been probably made aware of your strengths as a leader. I would like you to focus on these first before you consider a plan of action for your development as a leader.

Activities to identify and build on your strengths

Take a piece of paper and write a list of what your strengths are as a leader

Write your strengths in the present tense, using positive language, such as 'I am approachable', 'I am respectful of others' or 'I communicate clearly'.

When you've done this, underline your key strength as a leader. Consider how you can build on this strength. What can you do to use this strength more frequently in your current role? Consider how you can use this strength to help you become more effective as a leader.

For example, one leader of an IT department that I know is a great listener. In her leadership role, she realised that she could use this strength more to act as a mediator between her team and a key stakeholder group who were dissatisfied with an aspect of the service the department provided. She also recognised that she could coach her team more using this strength, in order to help them develop.

Visualise yourself being successful

The ability to see yourself doing things well programmes the mind to put those steps into action – the mind is suggestible.

Think of an occasion or situation where you were using your key strengths as a leader. Now close your eyes and watch yourself in this situation. Consider:

- Where you are.
- Who is in the audience or who is with you.
- What you are saying and doing.
- How you are looking – how you are dressed and presented.
- The positive reactions from others to what you are saying and doing.
- The way you are handling the group – your words, your tone and your body language.

Play this tape over several times in your mind, making the picture clearer and clearer each time. Notice the physiological changes as you do this and how much more positive you feel.

Play the images over again just before you feel you may be faced with a difficult situation as a leader and your confidence will undoubtedly increase.

Effective leaders share their passions

Think about what you are passionate about or what you love to do. If you have lost touch with what those are, write down what you were passionate about in the past. Think about a future occasion as a leader where you can bring this passion into your work. For example, as part of a team meeting you could spend some time on getting to know your team better, and on them getting to know you better, by all sharing something that you are passionate about or that inspires you.

Ask the team (include yourself in this) to bring with them to the team meeting something that symbolises what they are passionate about or what inspires them. Check beforehand that team members are willing to do this. This could be an object, a photo, a piece of music or a film clip, for example.

In a relaxed atmosphere, ask each team member to answer the following questions:

- What is your inspiration?
- Why did your example inspire you?
- What were the feelings you experienced at the time?
- What was the emotional impact of your inspiration and what did it cause you to do as a result?

Share your own passion or inspiration with the team too.

Creating a development plan as a leader

Having recognised your strengths, consider where you can develop further as a leader.

In order for you to create your own leadership capability development plan, here is the process that I recommend you undertake.

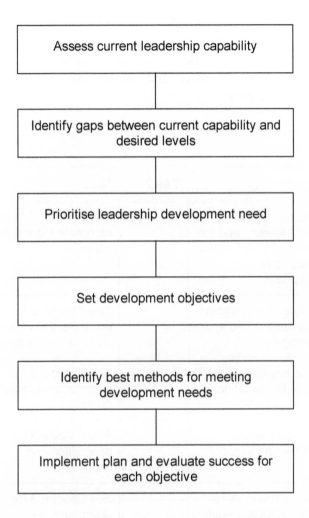

Figure 16: Leadership capability development plan process

This involves you assessing your leadership capability, identifying gaps, setting clear objectives for your personal development and deciding how you can address these.

7: Action Planning

In this book I have provided you with guidance on a wide range of leadership topics. I suggest that you use the following checklist to help you assess where your strengths are overall as a leader and where are your potential development areas.

	Yes?	No?
The amount of time that I spend leading and the amount of time I spend managing is appropriate		*See Chapter 1* for ideas on how to redress this balance
My style of leadership is both supportive and challenging		*See Chapter 2* for ideas on leadership styles and their implications
I adapt my leadership style to the situation and to the person		*See Chapter 2* for information on how to do this
I am politically intelligent as a leader		*See Chapter 3* for description and implications
I have a strong sense of my personal values and what I stand for		*See Chapter 3* for description and implications
I have good business knowledge (BQ)		*See Chapter 3* for description and implications

I am aware of my own emotions and of the emotions of others around me (EQ)		*See Chapter 3* for description and implications
I have set and regularly communicate a clear vision, goals and strategy for my team		*See Chapter 4* for information on how to do this
I have a powerful presence and make a positive impact		*See Chapter 5* for description and implications
I influence others effectively		*See Chapter 5* for information on how to do this
I create an environment which encourages empowerment		*See Chapter 6* for information on how to do this
I delegate appropriately		*See Chapter 6* for information on how to do this

Table 9: Leadership capability self-assessment

As you will see from the table, I have highlighted the chapters that provide the relevant information.

Creating a personal development plan

Once you have identified the gaps that you would like to fill, I recommend that you create a personal development plan to help you address these. Table 10 is a template that you can use to record your plan.

Development area to be addressed	Development objective (ensure that this is SMART)	Method you will use for development	Measures of success	When you will review progress?
E.g. increase percentage of time spent leading rather than managing	Increase time spent from 30% to 50% by the end of June this year	One-to-one coaching	Team score for sense of direction as measured by employee survey will increase from 55% to 85%	Interim review March, end review June

Table 10: Example of personal development plan

This will allow you to define:

- The leadership development area you wish to address.
- A development objective that is SMART: Specific, Measurable, Achievable, Realistic and Timebound.
- The method you will use for development.
- Your measures of success.
- When you will review progress.

There are a wide range of development options that you can use to improve your confidence and competence. These include:

- further reading
- workshops
- e-learning
- viewing DVDs
- assignments
- projects
- mentoring
- one-to-one coaching.

I suggest that you speak to your learning and development department or human resources business partner, who should be able to help you select the best development method to meet your needs.

Summary

In this final chapter I have outlined some methods to help you recognise your strengths as a leader and identify development areas. I have also encouraged you to create a personal development plan to increase your leadership capability.

Here are some questions to ask yourself:

- What do other people see as your key strengths as a leader?
- What do others view as your development areas?
- How can you supplement any existing feedback you have about you as a leader to ensure that you gain a rounded perspective?
- What does success, for you as a leader, look like?
- What will be a milestone for you as a leader?

GLOSSARY

Active listening: the skill of listening attentively to the speaker, of giving them your undivided attention, repeating their words and summarising what they say.

Aggressive behaviour: behaviour of someone that is based on the premise that they are more important than the person that they are interacting with, and which demonstrates a lack of respect towards them through their words, tone and body language.

Assertive behaviour: behaviour of someone who communicates their views, feelings and opinions in a confident and respectful manner, and who acts in a way which demonstrates that they consider themselves and the other person as equals.

Brainstorming: the act of generating a large number of ideas without evaluating them, letting one idea bounce off another in order to generate a wide range of options.

Business intelligence: having the foresight to envision the future and the drive to move the business forward.

Congruent: where the words, tone of voice and body language an individual is using all match one another.

Developmental feedback: providing feedback to an individual on where they could improve and develop.

Distributed leadership: leadership that is demonstrated at every level throughout the business.

Emotional intelligence: the ability to recognise your own and others' feelings and build strong, trusting relationships.

Mentoring: where a person shares their experience and knowledge with a junior person in order to help them grow and develop.

Non-assertive behaviour: behaviour of someone that is based on the premise that they and the person that they are interacting with are not equals. As a result, the individual is either not confident in expressing their thoughts and opinions, or is over-confident and disrespectful of the other person.

Passive behaviour: behaviour someone that is based on the premise that the person they are interacting with is superior to them. The result is that the individual does not express their own needs, wants and concerns during the interaction.

Political intelligence: knowing the bases of power in your organisation, who to influence and how.

SMART objective: an objective that is Specific, Measurable, Achievable, Realistic and Timebound. For example, in contrast to the objective 'to look at the glossary', a SMART objective would be 'to read this page within five minutes today'.

Spiritual intelligence: knowing who you are and what you believe, and having a sense of purpose.

BIBLIOGRAPHY

W. Bennis, *On Becoming a Leader*, Arrow, 1998, ISBN 0-201-08059-1

R. R. Blake and J. S. Mouton, *The Managerial Grid*, Gulf Publishing, 1964, ISBN 978-0-884152-52-1

R. R. Blake and J. S. Mouton, *The New Managerial Grid*, Gulf Publishing, 1978, ISBN 978-0-872014-73-2

S. Cook, S. Macaulay and H. Coldicott, *Effective Change Management*, Kogan Page, 2004, ISBN 978-0-749440-33-6

S. R. Covey, *The Seven Habits of Highly Effective People*, The Free Press, 2004, ISBN 0-7432-6951-9

J. Gardner, *On Leadership*, Free Press, 1993, ISBN 978-0-029113-12-7

D. Goleman, *Working with Emotional Intelligence*, Bloomsbury, 1999, ISBN 0-553-37858-9

P. Hersey, *The Situational Leader*, Pfeiffer and Co, 1984, ISBN 978-0-317139-71-6

P. Hersey and K. H. Blanchard, *The Management of Organizational Behaviour*, 8th edition, Prentice Hall, 2000, ISBN 978-0-130175-98-4

P. M. Senge, *The Fifth Discipline: The Art and Practice of the Learning Organization*, Random House, 1990, ISBN 0-385-51725-4

ITG RESOURCES

IT Governance Ltd sources, creates and delivers products and services to meet the real-world, evolving IT governance needs of today's organisations, directors, managers and practitioners. The ITG website (*www.itgovernance.co.uk*) is the international one-stop-shop for corporate and IT governance information, advice, guidance, books, tools, training and consultancy.

IT Governance products are also available, in local currencies, through

www.itgovernanceusa.com, and

www.itgovernanceasia.com.

Pocket Guides

For full details of the entire range of pocket guides, simply follow the links at *www.itgovernance.co.uk/publishing.aspx*.

Toolkits

ITG's unique range of toolkits includes the IT Governance Framework Toolkit, which contains all the tools and guidance that you will need in order to develop and implement an appropriate IT governance framework for your organisation. Full details are at *www.itgovernance.co.uk/products/519*.

For a free paper on how to use the proprietary CALDER-MOIR IT Governance Framework, and for a free trial version of the toolkit, see *www.itgovernance.co.uk/calder_moir.aspx*.

Best Practice Reports

ITG's new range of Best Practice Reports is now at: *www.itgovernance.co.uk/best-practice-reports.aspx*.   These offer you essential, pertinent, expertly researched information on an increasing number of key issues.

Training and Consultancy

IT Governance also offers training and consultancy services across the entire spectrum of disciplines in the information governance arena. Details of training courses can be accessed at *www.itgovernance.co.uk/training.aspx* and descriptions of our consultancy services can be found at *http://www.itgovernance.co.uk/consulting.aspx*.

Why not contact us to see how we could help you and your organisation?

Newsletter

IT governance is one of the hottest topics in business today, not least because it is also the fastest-moving, so what better way to keep up than by subscribing to ITG's free monthly newsletter *Sentinel*? It provides monthly updates and resources across the whole spectrum of IT governance subject matter, including risk management, information security, ITIL and IT service management, project governance, compliance and so much more. Subscribe for your free copy at: *www.itgovernance.co.uk/newsletter.aspx*.